THE COMIC BOOK BIBLE
FROM JACOB TO MOSES
Published by Scandinavia Publishing House 2012
Scandinavia Publishing House, Drejervej 15,3, DK-2400 Copenhagen, NV, Denmark
info@scanpublishing.dk
www.scanpublishing.dk

Concept by Jose Perez Montero
Text copyright © Ben Alex
Illustrations copyright © Jose Perez Montero
Design by Ben Alex
Printed in China
Hardcover ISBN 978 87 7132 053 4
Softcover ISBN 978 87 7132 052 7
All rights reserved

THE COMIC BOOK BIBLE

FROM JACOB TO MOSES

CONCEPT AND ILLUSTRATIONS BY JOSE PEREZ MONTERO

TEXT BY BEN ALEX

scandinavia

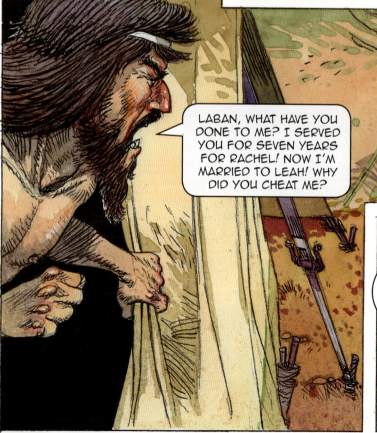

JACOB WORKS FOR LABAN   Genesis 29:22 – Genesis 30:43

For another seven years, Jacob worked for Laban.

Leah felt sad that Jacob didn't love her the same way he loved her sister Rachel. But God showed mercy on Leah. He gave her four sons -- Reuben, Simeon, Levi, and Judah. Rachel had no children at all.

Rachel and Leah thought Jacob would love them according to how many children they gave him.

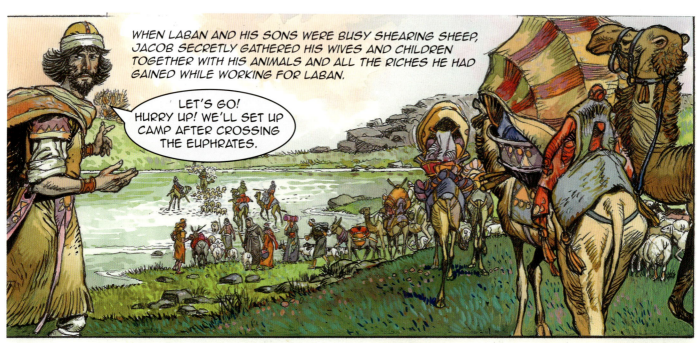

JACOB'S JOURNEY HOME   Genesis 31:1 – Genesis 35:29

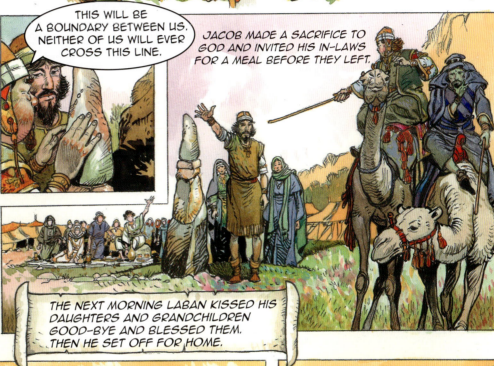

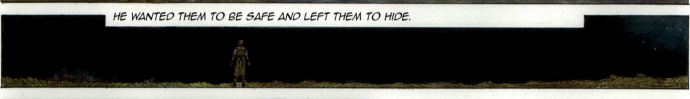

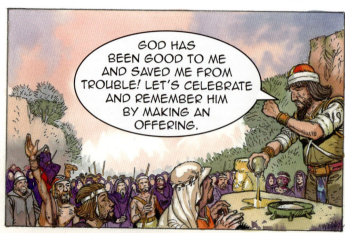

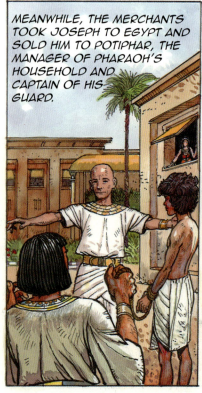

JOSEPH IN EGYPT Genesis 39:1 – Genesis 45:28

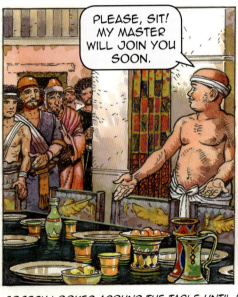

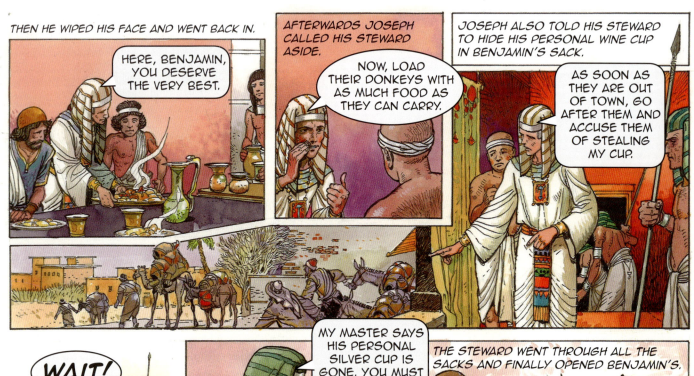

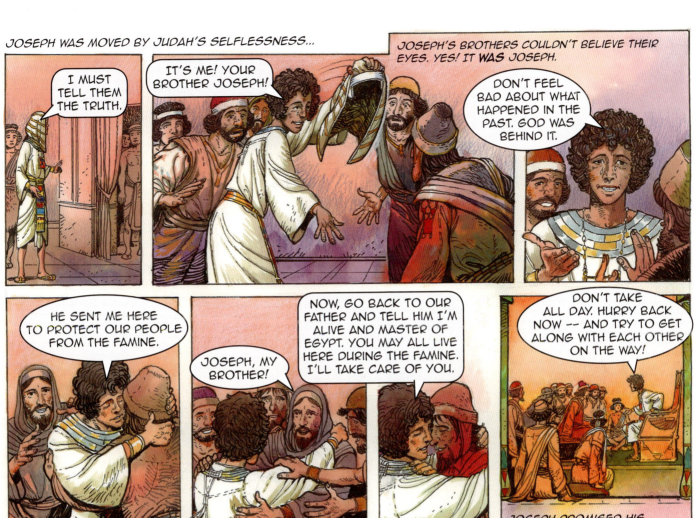
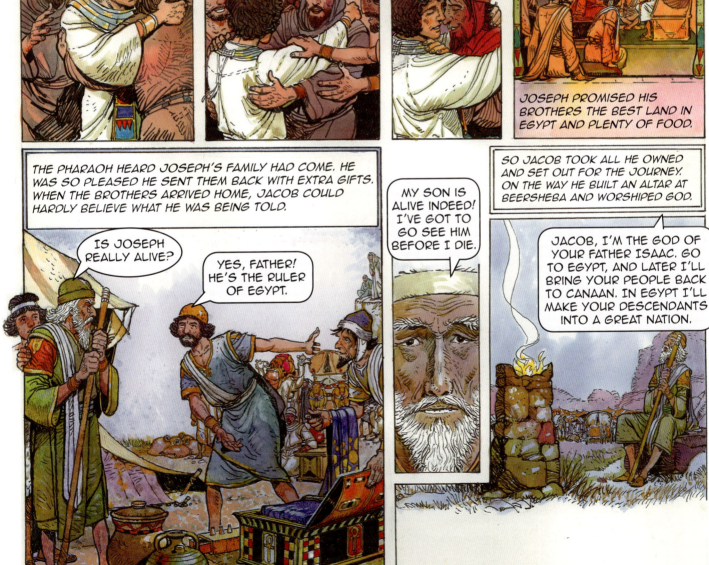

THE HEBREWS IN EGYPT — Genesis 46:1 – Exodus 1:14

22

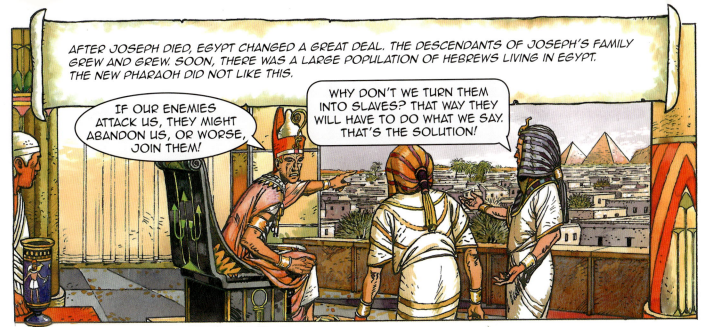

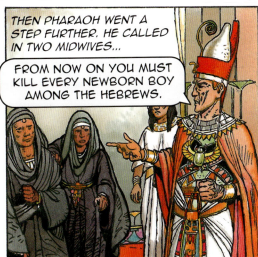

MOSES Exodus 1:15 – Exodus 4:30

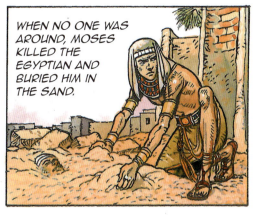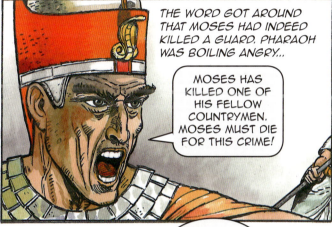

"LET MY PEOPLE GO!" Exodus 5:1 – Exodus 12:30

28

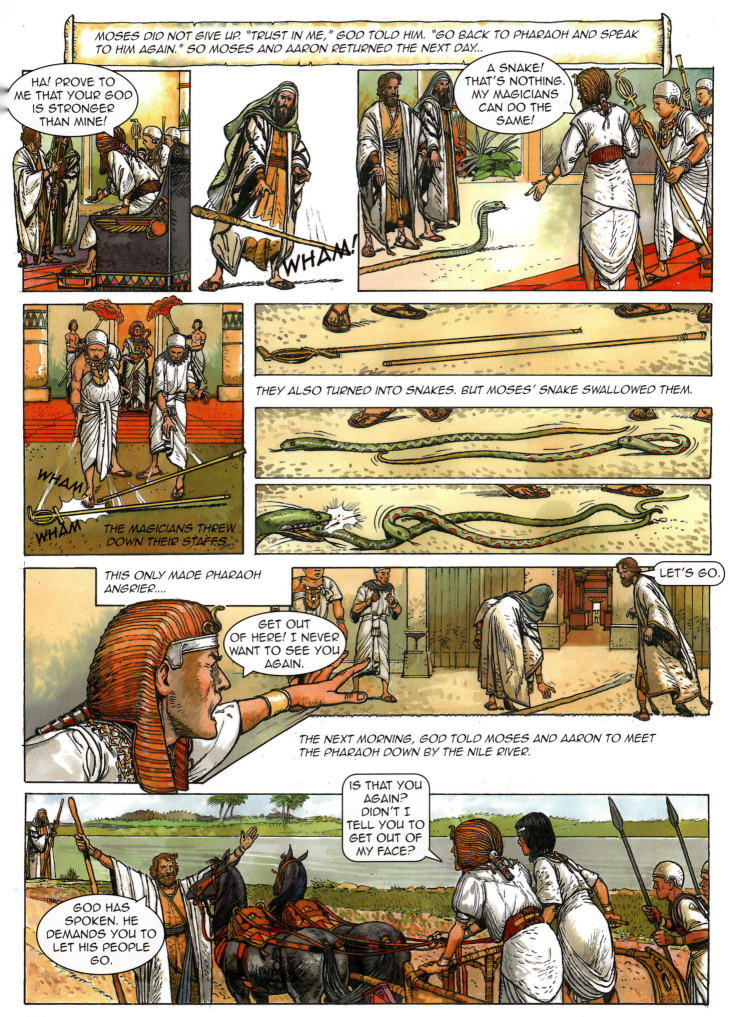

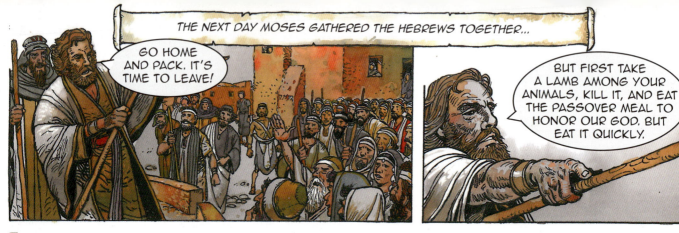

MOSES DID EXACTLY AS GOD HAD TOLD HIM. SOON A MIGHTY EAST WIND SWEPT OVER THE DESERT AND MADE THE SEA PART.

GO ON AND CROSS OVER! GOD WILL BE WITH US!

THE ISRAELITES HURRIED ACROSS THE SEABED WITH THE EGYPTIANS ON THEIR HEELS. BUT GOD CAUSED THE EGYPTIANS TO PANIC AS THEIR CHARIOT WHEELS SUNK IN THE WET SAND.

OH NO!

WE'RE STUCK!

GOD SAID TO MOSES, "IF YOU LISTEN CAREFULLY TO ME AND OBEY MY WORD, I'LL CERTAINLY NOT SMITE YOU WITH DISEASE LIKE I DID THE EGYPTIANS. I'LL TAKE CARE OF YOU. I'LL BE YOUR HEALER."

THE PEOPLE TRAVELED ON, AND THEY BELIEVED GOD WOULD PROVIDE FOR THEM IN THE WILDERNESS. HE CERTAINLY DID. THEY SET UP CAMP AT ELIM -- AN OASIS WITH TWELVE SPRINGS OF WATER AND 70 PALM TREES AROUND.

INTO THE DESERT Exodus 15:22 – Exodus 18:27

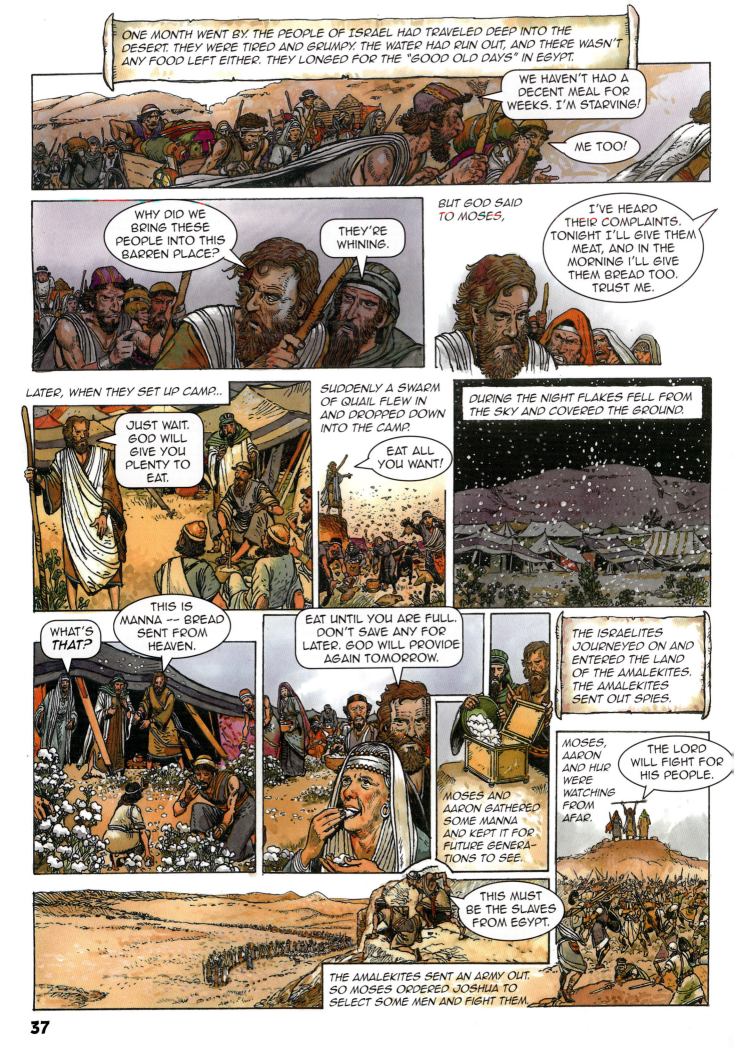

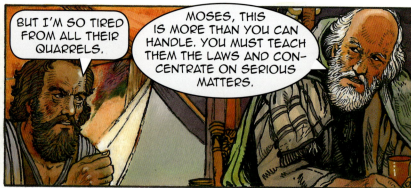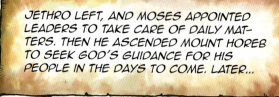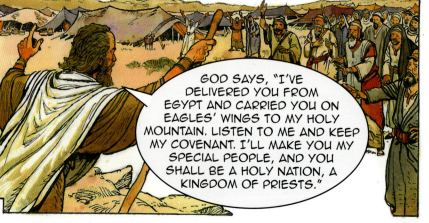

THE MOUNTAIN OF GOD — Exodus 19:1 – Leviticus 27:34

ON THE THIRD DAY, A STRONG WIND BEGAN TO BLOW. MOSES CLIMBED MT. SINAI TO MEET THE LORD.

THE STORM GREW WORSE, AND THE PEOPLE COWERED BELOW THE MOUNTAIN. THEY WATCHED IN AMAZEMENT AS THE MOUNTAIN WENT UP IN FLAMES.

BUT MOSES WAS NOT AFRAID.

"I TRUST YOU, GOD."

MOSES CONTINUED ALONE.

THEN GOD TOLD MOSES THE TEN COMMANDMENTS.

"WORSHIP ONLY ME! DO NOT WORSHIP STATUES! DON'T TAKE MY NAME IN VAIN! KEEP THE SABBATH SACRED!"

"HONOR YOUR PARENTS! DO NOT KILL! KEEP YOUR MARRIAGE PROMISES! DO NOT STEAL! DO NOT LIE! DO NOT COVET!"

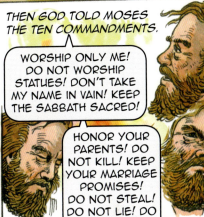

MOSES AND AARON CAME BACK DOWN THE MOUNTAIN. THEIR FACES WERE RADIANT WITH THE LIGHT OF GOD.

MOSES TOLD THE PEOPLE EVERYTHING THE LORD HAD SAID. THE NEXT MORNING HE INSTRUCTED THEM TO BUILD AN ALTAR AND MAKE SACRIFICES TO GOD. THEN HE SPRINKLED BLOOD FROM THE ANIMALS ON THE PEOPLE.

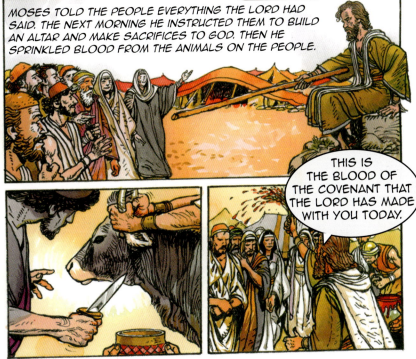

"TELL US WHAT GOD SAID! WE'LL OBEY EVERY WORD!"

"THIS IS THE BLOOD OF THE COVENANT THAT THE LORD HAS MADE WITH YOU TODAY."

AGAIN MOSES WENT UP TO MEET WITH GOD. THIS TIME HE BROUGHT HIS ASSISTANT JOSHUA TOGETHER WITH AARON, NADAB, ABIHU, AND SEVENTY ELDERS. ON THE MOUNTAIN THEY SAW GOD IN HIS GLORY -- SHINING LIKE GOLD AND BRIGHT AS THE CLEAR SKY. THEY FEASTED TOGETHER IN GOD'S PRESENCE.

MOSES TOLD AARON AND THE ELDERS TO GO BACK AND TAKE CARE OF THE PEOPLE. BUT HE KEPT JOSHUA WITH HIM AND CLIMBED THE MOUNTAIN AGAIN.

JOSHUA, WAIT HERE!

THE CLOUD OF GOD'S GLORY COVERED THE MOUNTAIN. MOSES WENT INTO THE CLOUD.

IN THE MEANTIME, THE PEOPLE WERE WAITING AT THE FOOT OF THE MOUNTAIN.

MOSES HAS BEEN GONE FOR SEVERAL WEEKS.

WE CAN'T WAIT FOREVER! HE MAY BE DEAD. AARON, MAKE US A NEW GOD!

NO WAY!

AFTER SIX DAYS THE LORD SPOKE TO MOSES AGAIN...

MOSES, I'LL WRITE MY COMMANDMENTS ON TABLETS OF STONE SO THE PEOPLE WON'T FORGET THEM.

COME CLOSER!

THERE GOD GAVE MOSES THE LAW. MEANWHILE...

AARON TRIED TO CALM THE PEOPLE...

BE PATIENT, MY FRIENDS. GOD KNOWS WHAT HE'S DOING.

BUT FINALLY HE GAVE IN...

WE'RE LOST IN THIS DESERT WITHOUT A GOD TO PROTECT US!

OK, THEN. BRING ME ALL THE GOLD JEWELRY YOU CAN GET!

HERE ARE MY COMMANDS TO YOU AND THE PEOPLE OF ISRAEL.

MOSES PICKED UP THE TABLETS OF STONE.

DOWN BELOW, AARON MADE A CALF IDOL OUT OF THE GOLD. HE ALSO BUILT AN ALTAR IN FRONT OF THE IDOL AND URGED THE PEOPLE TO WORSHIP THE LORD.

40

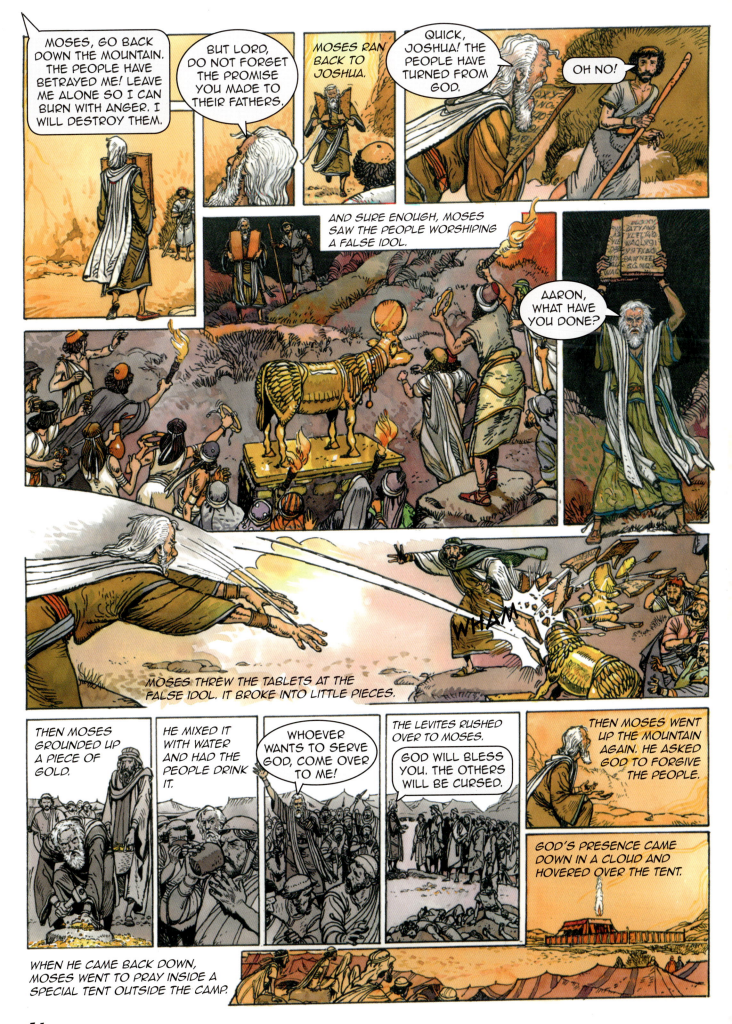

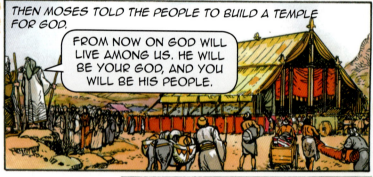

TOWARDS THE PROMISED LAND Numbers 10:11 – Deuteronomy 34:12

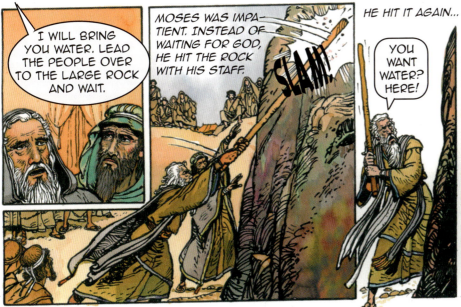